# Introduct

**T**he Vale of Glamorgan is the broa( farmland between Cardiff and Bridg the dramatic coastline around the so stretches for about 35 miles from Cardiff Bay covers all this length. The 14 mile central section, between Aberthaw and Porthcawl, was designated as a Heritage Coast in 1973.

The cliffs along this coast are made up of an unusual layering of limestone and shale. This creates some remarkable and photogenic rock formations. Years of erosion has also had an impact on the shore below, forming shingle shelves and sandbanks out from the cliff base into the sea. Nash Lighthouse and other shipping protection bear witness to the coast's potential for danger. Beyond the relatively few honeypots, the coast is often deserted. For its entire length the seascape offers wide views across the Bristol Channel. On a clear day the hills of Exmoor and the landscape of Somerset and Devon form a backdrop to the sea.

**Walks are divided into two groups:**

**Walks 1–11** are lineal and circular routes that cover the Coast Path for the whole of its length along the Glamorgan coast – from Cardiff Bay to Kenfig Dunes. They can be walked as individual days out, or joined together as a guide to a Coast Path expedition. They are organised from east to west. There is a paragraph at the end of each of these walks outlining the Coast Path itinerary and summarising the link to the next walk where there is a gap.

The Wales Coast Path extends for 870 miles from the Wye to the Dee and offers intense variety, dramatic geology and scenic beauty. Most of the path in this region is easy to follow. The hinterland of the Glamorgan coast is largely arable farming, and can be subject to incursion by undergrowth. In the walks described I have opted for passable and clear routes on the assumption that you share my preference for walking rather than jungle warfare. Of course, things can change!

**Walks 12–20** include a variety of other circular routes in coastal and inland locations across the Vale of Glamorgan and Cardiff.

There are frequent trains between Cardiff, Penarth and Barry and an hourly service on to Rhoose, Llantwit Major and Bridgend. There is also a regular bus service near the coast between Barry and Bridgend. Further detail is included in each walk. There is a huge amount to explore here, and many surprises in store, including the largest dune system in Europe between Ogmore and Kenfig (**Walks 10, 16 & 17**). Nature and geology is unpacked by the Glamorgan Heritage Coast Centre at Dunraven Bay (**Walks 9 & 14**) while history and heritage await exploration at the St Fagan's National History Museum (**Walk 20**) or Llandaff (Walk 19). There are country parks with many more alternative walking options at Porthkerry (**Walks 4 & 12**) and Cosmeston (**Walk 2**).

So enjoy the variety, the scenery and the bracing Atlantic air!

# ACROSS CARDIFF BAY

**DESCRIPTION** Building the barrage across Cardiff Bay impounded a huge freshwater pool collecting waters from the Rivers Taff and Ely. The structure itself is just over ½ mile long and was completed in 1999. Although environmentally controversial, the whole project has had enormous impact on the regeneration of the old Cardiff docklands. The walkway to Penarth only dates from 2008. The route offers a shortcut of 2 miles and stupendous views across Cardiff and the Bristol Channel.

This walk takes the eastern side of the Bay from the Pier Head to Penarth, crossing the barrage and sea locks. From the Custom House, a short climb leads to the Victorian resort of Penarth, crowning a sandstone ridge. From here there are buses and trains back to Cardiff. A waterbus service also provides an alternative route back to Cardiff from the Custom House.

It is possible to follow the whole Cardiff Bay Trail, a circular 6-mile route for walkers and cyclists. This traces the rim of the Bay beyond the Custom House and back to Cardiff, but this is better for cyclists than walkers.

**DISTANCE AND TERRAIN** Linear walk: 2 miles in single direction. Use bus, train or boat as an alternative to walking back. Excellent surfaced paths with just one short climb into Penarth. No shortage of shops, cafes and other refreshment places in Cardiff and Penarth. There are toilets at a number of places en route.

**START** Pier Head Building, opposite the National Assembly of Wales. Pay and display parking in the area– or use bus or train. Post code: CF10 4PH. Grid ref: ST 193745.

Cardiff Bay is a mile from the City Centre, following Lloyd George Avenue. Frequent bus service (No 6, 'Bay Car') from the City Centre and the back of Central Station. Cardiff Bay Station is ¼ m from the Pier Head on foot.

**1** The red brick Pier Head building is now used by the National Assembly but it started life as railway and dock offices. With the building behind you, turn left to follow the dual-use walk and cycle path along the edge of the bay, passing the white wooden Norwegian arts centre and coffee shop. *This was originally the Scandinavian seamen's church and was transported from Norway in the middle of the nineteenth century. Roald Dahl was baptised here.* Continue across the lock into Roath Basin, following signs for the Cardiff Bay Trail all around. *The trail deviates left around the Doctor Who Experience, a major pilgrimage destination, with special effects, props and artefacts from the cult science fiction epic.* Continue along the side of the Bay, passing a sailing centre and skate board park to reach the edge of the Bristol Channel.

*The Barrage now lies ahead with the rocky bluff of Penarth rearing up beyond, crowned by the spire of St Augustine's Church. The hills of Somerset loom across the Channel, with the contrasting islands of Flat Holm (in Wales) and Steep Holm (in England) in the foreground. The Captain Scott Exhibition is just off the path to the right. The British Antarctic Survey expedition to the South Pole set sail from Cardiff in 1910, led by Captain Robert Scott. Although five men, led by Scott, reached the Pole, they met their deaths on the return leg in ferocious weather.*

Cross the Barrage and the three sea locks to arrive at the Penarth Custom House, built in 1865, now a restaurant. There is a regular Waterbus service from here to various points around the Bay and back to the Pier Head. There are also seasonal trips to Flat Holm.

**2** At this point leave the Cardiff Bay Trail and continue diagonally up the hill on Paget Road. Towards the top bear left at a triangular junction but then bear right and continue uphill along Maughan Terrace. Beyond here follow Stanwell Crescent and Albert Road into the centre of Penarth. It is possible to follow a number of alternative routes into the town centre. *Victorian buildings lend an air of elegance to Penarth, supplemented by attractive gardens, a historic pier and a popular esplanade.*

Frequent buses run from here back to Cardiff or on to Barry. The railway station lies a little further along Stanwell Road, just past the centre of town, with a regular service to Cardiff.

## Wales Coast Path: Stage I
## Cardiff Bay to Penarth

Most of this route coincides with the Wales Coast Path. The official route diverges just after the Penarth Custom House at Point 2 to take a more circuitous route around suburban roads. Unless you want to follow the pure route, you could just as well follow Walk 1 to its conclusion in the centre of Penarth and continue on Walk 2. This begins at Penarth Railway Station and re-joins the Coast Path at the Pier to follow the next stage to Lavernock Point.

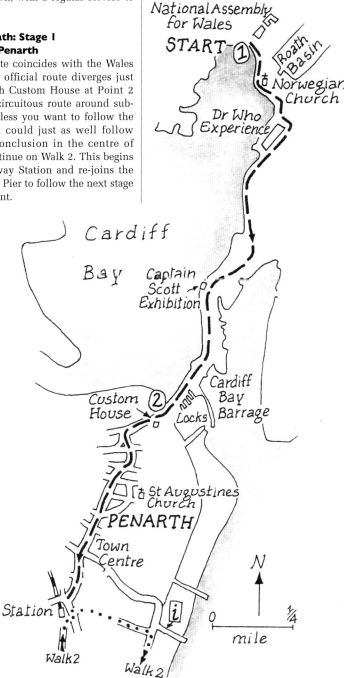

# PENARTH, LAVERNOCK & COSMESTON LAKES

**DESCRIPTION** Penarth has always been a popular excursion from Cardiff and the valleys, its Victorian facades and teashops offering a rather more genteel appeal than the funfair and candy floss of Barry Island. The town commands a sandstone cliff guarding the entrance to Cardiff Bay. There are wide views across the sea from the town on the first section of this walk. There is also plenty of history, with the site of the first radio signal across water at Lavernock and a rebuilt medieval settlement at Cosmeston. One other bonus of this walk – it's nearly all flat.

The outward stretch follows the Wales Coast Path along the cliffs to Lavernock Point with open views across the Bristol Channel and back to Cardiff. From Lavernock, a quiet lane leads to the country park at Cosmeston Lakes. The park includes two lakes, woodland walks and abundant bird life. A reconstructed medieval village is open to visitors. The return route to Penarth follows the line of the old railway from Barry.

**DISTANCE & TERRAIN** 5 miles, mostly level on paths, tracks and a section of quiet road. Shops, pubs, cafés in Penarth town centre. Café, visitor centre and toilets at Cosmeston Lake.

**START** Penarth Railway Station. Post code: CF64 3EE. Grid ref: ST 185714. The walk could also begin at Cosmeston Lakes Visitor Centre (Point 6) on the B4267 just outside the edge of Penarth.

**DIRECTIONS** Reach Penarth by the A4160 from Cardiff or the B4267 from Barry. There are frequent trains to Penarth from Cardiff Queen Street and Cardiff Central. Regular buses run from Cardiff city centre and Barry.

**I** The walk starts from the other side of the track from the station entrance and ticket office, so if arriving by train, walk up the ramp to the road and cross back over the railway bridge. At the far side of the bridge, at the junction with traffic lights, turn right onto Plymouth Road for 100 yards before turning left to follow a footpath signed to the Esplanade. This goes downhill between the Glendale Hotel and Turner House Gallery, following a small ravine. The path crosses this half way down, with Alexandra Park on the left. When the path ends continue downhill on a road to reach the Pier. *The Pavilion was restored in 2013 and the Pier is a great place to enjoy an ice cream or coffee.*

**2** Turn right and follow the Esplanade, which is also the Wales Coast Path, past the lifeboat station and then up Cliff Hill. At the top of the hill, bear left by the shelter, following the Coast Path. Continue along the top of the cliffs on the popular track. If the weather is clear, spot the islands in the Bristol Channel and the coast of Somerset. At the end of the built-up area, continue through a gate to follow the Coast Path along the cliff and between hedges for the best part of a mile.

**3** Arriving at the houses next to Lavernock Point, turn right through a gate on to a lane. Pass a chapel on the right. *There is plaque embedded in the wall, marking an important experiment in wireless technology. It was here, in 1897, that Guglielmo Marconi received the first wireless transmission across water, from Flat Holm, around two miles away to the south east.* Continue along the lane, passing a holiday park and the entrance to Lavernock Point Nature Reserve.

**4** Keep going for another half mile to reach a busy main road.

**5** Cross the road and go over a stile opposite, following a path across the next small field. To the right is the reconstructed medieval village. At the end of the field go through a gate and turn right, following a track between the two lakes. Cross a bridge and then turn right, taking a path above the shore of the eastern lake and on to the Visitor Centre. *Refreshments, toilets and information are all here. Visitors are also welcome in the medieval village, an archaeological recon-*

*struction of a 14thC Anglo-Welsh community. A number of different buildings and gardens have been recreated and there is also a small museum.*

**6** From the Visitor Centre, pass through the car park and cross the main road near the bus stop. Follow the main road left for a short distance and then turn right along Falcon Grove into a housing estate. After about 350 yards, next to Althorp Drive, turn left along a dual-use path and cycleway. This follows the line of the railway to Barry via Sully, now truncated at Penarth. The track returns to the station, around 1¼ miles away. As it approaches the station, a path veers to the right, and then back to the left, avoiding a residential home, before arriving back at the station.

### Wales Coast Path: Stage 2
### Penarth to Lavernock
The Path is followed between Penarth Pier and Lavernock, as far as Point 4. To continue on the Coast Path, leave this walk at Point 4 and pick up Walk 3 at Point 2, continuing to Sully and Barry.

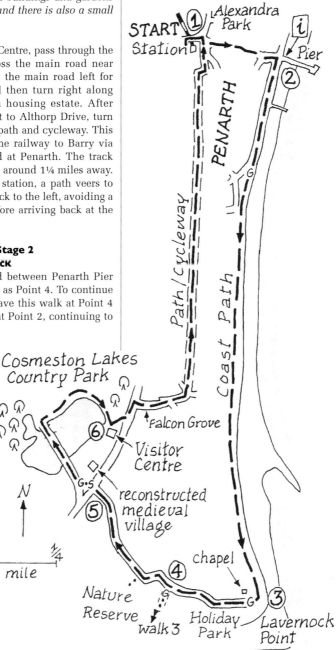

# LAVERNOCK NATURE RESERVE & SULLY ISLAND

**DESCRIPTION** The coast makes a full right-angle turn at Lavernock Point, turning its back on the capital. Here begins the great south-facing seaboard of Wales, looking west towards the Glamorgan Heritage Coast. Despite the proximity of urban areas, the section of coastline between Penarth and Sully offers an attractive and interesting route, with picturesque nooks and fantastic views.

This is presented as a linear route and the return trip makes an excellent outing with contrasting views. Alternatively, there is a regular bus service along the road from Swanbridge to Cosmeston and Penarth. It is also possible to vary the return by walking along the lane to the hamlet of Cog and then turning right along a field path to Cosmeston, though parts of this are hard to follow.

**DISTANCE & TERRAIN**
Linear walk – 2½ miles each way, including optional extension to Sully Island. Undulating paths though nature reserve and alongside fields, with sections of walking on quiet lanes. The crossing to Sully Island is on a tidal rock causeway. Timing is very important! Consult tide times and advice displayed at Swanbridge. Cosmeston Lake has a café, visitor centre and toilets. There is a pub at Swanbridge.

**START** Cosmeston Lakes Visitor Centre. Post code: CF64 5UY. Grid ref: ST 178692.

**DIRECTIONS** The Park is on the B4267 between Penarth and Sully. There is a regular bus service between Cardiff and Barry via Sully (94) which stops on the road outside.

**1** *Cosmeston is a 100 hectare country park with woods, lakes and reed beds. Since 2013 it has been a nature reserve. There are three waymarked routes through the park from 1¼ to 2½ miles in length. In one cor-ner of the park there is a reconstructed 14th century medieval village with barns, cottages and gardens. Scenes from the television programme Merlin were shot here.* From the car park, go past the warden's office, café and visitor centre towards the medieval village. Follow the boardwalks to the village. In front of the gates, turn right along the concrete track, to meet another track in about 300 yards. Turn left and follow this for about 100 yards before turning left again through a kissing gate. The footpath takes a short cut across a small field to reach the main road. Cross the road and continue on the lane opposite towards Lavernock village for about ½ mile.

**2** Just before the holiday park entrance, there is a gate and public footpath sign. *The Wales Coast Path is joined here.* Go through the gate and follow the path up the left hand side of the field on the boundary of the holiday camp. Continue along it through the Lavernock nature reserve along the top of the cliffs. Pass the remains of the Second World War anti-aircraft battery that guarded this section of coast. In ½ mile the path comes to the edge of the cliff by a lookout post overlooking St Mary's Well Bay. *Enjoy the view here.* However, after a pause, retrace a few steps to find the Coast Path continuing inland. (Although there is apparently a path on the cliff side of the caravan site, it is not a through route.) Unable or unwilling to climb down the rocks to the bay, the Coast Path takes a course around the caravan park. After a short woodland section it crosses a footbridge over a ditch and then climbs along the side of a couple of arable fields. At the top of the hill, turn left, going through a kissing gate to a reach a lane, next to the caravan site entrance.

**3** Bear left here and follow the public road, a narrow lane, downhill through the woods, passing Ball Bay and Ball Rock. There is no footpath but it's a cul-de-sac and not normally busy. It comes to an end at Swanbridge Farm but there is a pedestrian route through to another cul-de-sac at the Captain's Wife pub.

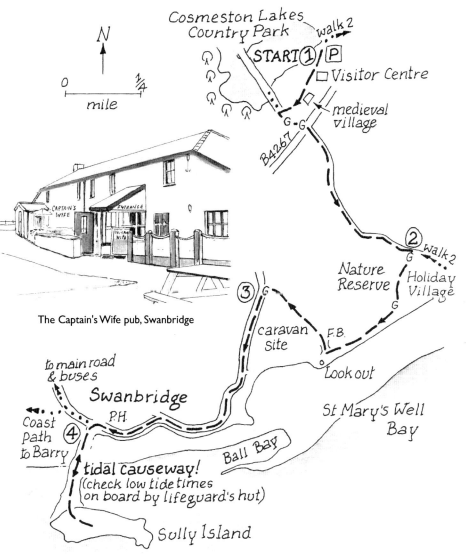

The Captain's Wife pub, Swanbridge

**4** From here a ¼ mile rocky causeway leads over to Sully Island. It is possible to cross this when the tide is low and times are shown on an indicator board on the lifeguard's hut. There is also a refreshment kiosk here. Care and common sense are of course needed, though in 2014 warning 'traffic' lights were also proposed! Sully Island is a small rocky and grassy island which is about ¼ mile long, rising to about 50 feet at its highest point.

## Wales Coast Path: Stage 3
## Lavernock to Sully

The Coast Path is picked up at Point 2. Follow this walk from Point 2 to Point 4 at Swanbridge. From here, it continues along the seaboard for another mile before turning inland to Sully. There is then a three mile urban section along the perimeter of Barry Docks until Barry railway station. Walk 4 starts here.

## WALK 4

# BARRY TO RHOOSE

**DESCRIPTION** An attractive and interesting segment of coast, making an easy and enjoyable linear walk. An hourly train service links the stations at either end. There are plenty of marks of human activity, from former limestone quarries to caravan sites, but these are interwoven with varied terrain, nature reserves and spectacular views.

**DISTANCE & TERRAIN** Linear walk, 5 miles in one direction, on an excellent, well-maintained path. Two steep but short climbs. All facilities in Barry. There is a café and toilets at Porthkerry Country Park.

**START** Barry Railway Station. Post code: CF62 8AF. Grid ref: ST 107673. (Don't confuse this with stations at Barry Docks or Barry Island.)

**DIRECTIONS** The station is on Broad St near the town centre. There are frequent trains and buses from Cardiff and an hourly service to Bridgend via Rhoose and Llantwit Major. Use the train to return from Rhoose or alternatively leave the car at Rhoose and catch the train back to start the walk.

**1** From the front of the station, turn left. After about 200 yards, bear left, crossing the railway, walking down to a mini-roundabout next to the Ship Inn. At the junction, the Coast Path official route offers a circuit of Barry Island. Otherwise, turn right, to walk along The Parade. Better still, walk through the pleasant gardens alongside. *On your left is the original harbour. This is now silted up, but the prostrate hulls of several beached vessels give a clue to former activity. Across the harbour the attractions of the Valleys' playground rise up on Barry Island.* At the end of the gardens, rejoin the road and then take the first left into Cold Knap Way. At the end, continue straight ahead down the wide footpath to reach Watch House Bay and Cold Knap Point, the more sedate and tranquil end of Barry. Turn right by the lifeguard station, or go straight across the park, to reach the opposite side of the little headland, off Cold Knap Point. If you like, do a circuit of the point itself. Walk along Cold Knap

Promenade, next to the raised shingle beach. Ahead, the bulk of Bull Cliff presages the westward coast of Glamorgan. The railway viaduct carries the Vale of Glamorgan line across the cleft at Porthkerry.

**2** Almost at the end of the promenade, follow the concrete footpath behind the

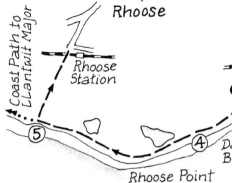

toilets, past some flats and the remains of Roman buildings preserved in a small enclosure. The path leads up the side of a grassy hill. After a short but steep climb, the route veers round to the left, following the edge of the grass. Now at the top of Bull Cliff, effort is rewarded with panoramic views across the Bristol Channel. Continue for nearly half a mile along the grass with houses on the top of the bank to the right. At the end of the section, the path dives straight ahead into the woods, tracing a route through Bull Cliff Wood, along the edge of a steep ridge between the sea and Porthkerry Country Park. The ridge comes to an end at a staircase, the Golden Steps, leading back down to the edge of a shingle beach. Cross a footbridge and divert inland to the café if you want a break.

**3** The path itself continues on the foreshore, just inland from the shingle beach. *A board warns of adders in the long grass!* Soon the path veers right off the foreshore and climbs steadily through sycamore wood to reclaim the cliff top. *In season, Speckled Wood butterflies flit across the path; ivy clings to the trees and the ground.* At the top, cross an open grass clearing, noting the lighting gantry for nearby Rhoose Airport.

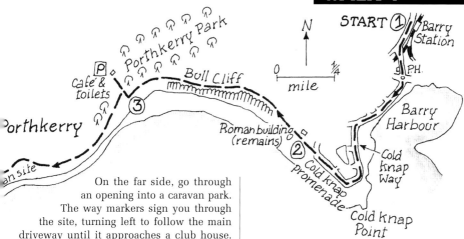

On the far side, go through an opening into a caravan park. The way markers sign you through the site, turning left to follow the main driveway until it approaches a club house. Turn right and take the roadway across the top of the site, before turning left above an old quarry, now inhabited by caravans. Just before the track dives down into the quarry itself, leave the site by taking a footpath doubling back to the right. The hedges on both sides disguise its position on a thin ridge of rock between two disused quarries. It curves round left, across a patch of open ground, then left again, before the first houses of Rhoose. Continue to follow the Coast Path as it weaves through woodland before at last regaining its proper cliff top course. The houses of Rhoose are not far to the right, but the path follows a lovely route, right on the edge of the cliff, the open heath studded with brambles and offering fantastic views across the Bristol Channel. *In season it is alive with limestone butterflies, such as the Common Blue.*

**4** After a while, you drop down some steps to a small valley at Dams Bay but the path continues straight ahead, up another flight of steps and on along the cliff top. *Later, on the right hand side, a lagoon is an indication of the extent and value of the limestone quarries along this coastline. You would slip obliviously past the most southerly mainland point in Wales, if it wasn't for the marker sign for Rhoose Point.* Just beyond, an upright obelisk, made of north Wales slate, also celebrates the geographical significance. Pass two great openings onto the shingle beach and then a further lagoon inland. About ½ mile after Rhoose Point, drop down another flight of steps to a small footbridge and come to a junction of paths.

**5** Leave the coast path here and turn right up the concrete path. Follow this for less than ¼ mile to reach Rhoose station.

## Wales Coast Path: Stage 4
## Barry to Summerhouse Point

This walk follows the route of the Coast Path for almost its entire length from Point 1 at Barry station to Point 5, just past Rhoose Point.

To continue on the Coast Path beyond Point 5, keep straight ahead. Pass another quarry and then a large caravan site at Fontygarry. At the far end, the Path leaves the site and drops down to the salt marsh. It goes just inside a sea wall before crossing the River Thaw. It then passes the huge complex of Aberthaw Power Station, past Breaksea Point and on to the small car park at Limpert. The Heritage Coast begins here and a direct route along the shore looks inviting. However, it is not recommended with huge boulders to negotiate and subject to dangerous tides. The official Coast Path route goes inland but is a difficult course. The ½ mile lane to Gileston is easy enough. The path turns left on entry to the village, taking a promising track. However, it soon deteriorates into field paths which are overgrown, obstructed and difficult before emerging back to the shore near Summerhouse Point.

# THE HERITAGE COAST AROUND LLANTWIT MAJOR

**DESCRIPTION** This route explores the coast and hinterland around Llantwit Major and Boverton. The coastal section links two Iron Age forts at Summerhouse Bay and Castle Ditches. For more information on Llantwit Major, see Walk 13.

**DISTANCE & TERRAIN** 6 miles. Walking is on lanes, cliff and field paths and an inevitable section of urban, though not unpleasant, walking at the start. No significant hills, though in high summer, crops may squeeze space on the Coast Path in places. All facilities are available in Llantwit. There is also a café and toilets at Cwm Colhuw beach.

**START** Car park next to the Town Hall, Burial Lane, Llantwit Major. Post code: CF61 1SD. Grid ref: SS 967687.

**DIRECTIONS** Llantwit Major is easily reached by road from Barry, Cowbridge and Bridgend. There is an hourly train service from Cardiff and Bridgend on the Vale of Glamorgan line. The station is a short walk from the Town Hall. There is also a regular bus service between Barry and Bridgend via Llantwit.

**I** Turn right out of the car park to follow Church Street. In a few yards, bear right into East Street, passing the White Lion. *This is Llantwit Major's main shopping street and there is also a small precinct to the left.* At the end, keep straight ahead at a mini-roundabout into Boverton Road. Continue along this road, passing turnings to the schools, leisure centre and cemetery and continuing into the neighbouring community of Boverton (Trebefered). In just over half a mile, at the bottom of a small hill, you come to a parade of shops on the right.

**2** Turn right here, next to the post office, up Tre-Berferad Road. *A few yards along this, on the left, a blue plaque commemorates Boverton Place, a ruined 16thC mansion built by Wales' leading lawyer, Roger Seys. The ruin looms above the village.* Shortly afterwards, take the first left along Mill Road, This tranquil lane leaves the built up area and continues between hedge lined arable fields towards the sea. In about ¾ mile the lane passes a group of refurbished cottages and buildings around Boverton Farm. Continue straight ahead for just under ½ mile until the lane ends at a small informal car park, marked with the sign, 'Summer House Point Promontory Fort'. At the side of the car park, follow the sign for the Sea Watch Centre and find a path running downhill between hedges. As it goes through the woods, it crosses a depression, colonised by hart's tongue fern. *This is one of the defensive ditches of the Celtic fort on this site.* Soon after, the path turns sharp right and comes to a junction.

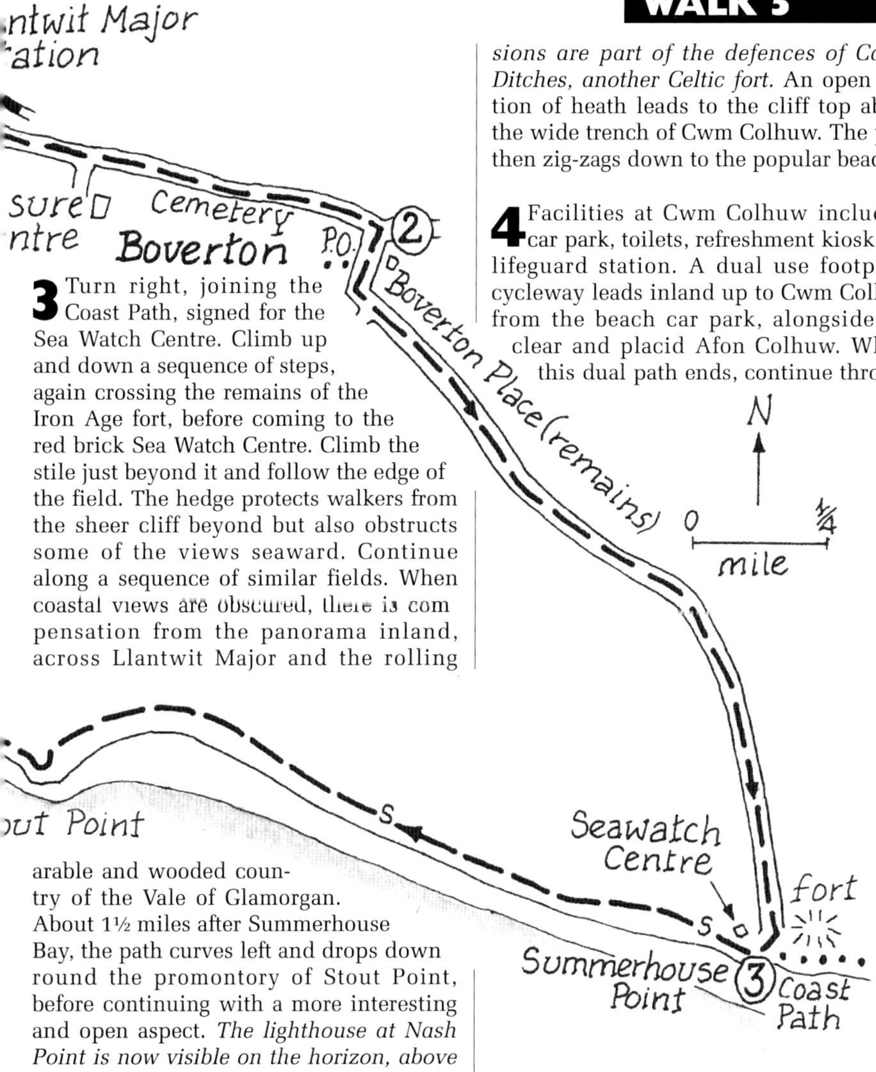

sions are part of the defences of Castle Ditches, another Celtic fort. An open section of heath leads to the cliff top above the wide trench of Cwm Colhuw. The path then zig-zags down to the popular beach.

**4** Facilities at Cwm Colhuw include a car park, toilets, refreshment kiosk and lifeguard station. A dual use footpath/cycleway leads inland up to Cwm Colhuw from the beach car park, alongside the clear and placid Afon Colhuw. Where this dual path ends, continue through

sure☐ Cemetery
ntre Boverton P.O.

**3** Turn right, joining the Coast Path, signed for the Sea Watch Centre. Climb up and down a sequence of steps, again crossing the remains of the Iron Age fort, before coming to the red brick Sea Watch Centre. Climb the stile just beyond it and follow the edge of the field. The hedge protects walkers from the sheer cliff beyond but also obstructs some of the views seaward. Continue along a sequence of similar fields. When coastal views are obscured, there is compensation from the panorama inland, across Llantwit Major and the rolling

N

0 ⅛ mile

ut Point

arable and wooded country of the Vale of Glamorgan. About 1½ miles after Summerhouse Bay, the path curves left and drops down round the promontory of Stout Point, before continuing with a more interesting and open aspect. *The lighthouse at Nash Point is now visible on the horizon, above the woods of St. Donat's (Walk 6). The whole expanse of the Bristol Channel lies in front. The cliffs ahead show the distinctive formation of this coastline. The layers of shale and carboniferous limestone almost give an appearance of intentional construction. Because shale is harder than limestone, the cliffs are geologically unstable and continue to crumble in the sea. Centuries of erosion have left shelves of rock and sand below. After an arable field, a gate leads to a corrugated section of land, overgrown by shrubs. These depres-*

Seawatch Centre

fort

Summerhouse Point ③ Coast Path

a gate, on to a footpath across a waterside meadow. At the far end of the meadow, go through a gate and turn left along a lane. Follow the road up into Llantwit Major, where it arrives close to the Town Hall.

**Wales Coast Path: Stage 5**
**Summerhouse Bay to Cwm Colhuw**
The Coast Path extends between Points 3 at Summerhouse Bay and Point 4 at Cwm Colhuw. To continue beyond Cwm Colhuw, go to the start of Walk 6 when you reach Point 4.

# NASH POINT & ST DONAT'S

**DESCRIPTION** The Glamorgan Heritage Coast offers fantastic views across the Bristol Channel and this section is no exception. The Coast Path reaches the landmark of Nash Point Lighthouse, before returning inland through the attractive village of Marcross. Later it passes through the interesting settlement of St Donat's, where a medieval castle and church lies cocooned in woodland, now largely a college campus.

**DISTANCE & TERRAIN** 7 miles, undulating coast path, with a few sections on quiet lanes and field paths. A few short climbs. The Beach Café is next to the car park at the start of the walk, where there are also toilets. There is a refreshment cabin at Nash Point and a pub at Marcross.

**START** Pay and display car park at Cwm Colhuw on the seashore near Llantwit Major. Post code: CF61 1RF. Grid ref: SS 957674

**DIRECTIONS** Cwm Colhuw is a mile from the centre of Llantwit Major. Follow Colhugh St from the town towards the sea shore. The railway station at Llantwit Major is served by an hourly train service connecting Cardiff, Barry and Bridgend. There is also a regular bus service between Barry and Bridgend via Llantwit Major.

**1** Climb the steps behind the lifeguard building to gain the cliff top. Once surmounted, keep left and follow the cliff path between hedges and undergrowth, looking ahead along the coast towards the woods and cliffs at St Donat's Point. *The views become ever more panoramic as the path crosses the open cliff top.* In ½ mile, cut down some steps to the little cove at Tresilian Bay before crossing a raised shingle beach.

**2** Climb the flight of steps on the opposite side of the cove to regain the cliff top. The way continues across a strip of land between the cliff top and fields. It turns sharply to the right just before some woods. Immediately after this right angle bend, turn left through a kissing gate and follow the coast path into the woods. Ignore a side turning to the beach, keeping to the high level coast path. Leaving the wood, the eclectic blend of edifices at St Donat's come into view across the fields. *The village is built around a 12thC castle and the grounds also include Atlantic College and a medieval church, passed on the return leg of the walk. St Donat himself came from the coast of Croatia.* A well-made hard core path now leads down through sycamore woods, passing on the coastal side of the college grounds, leading down to the sea at St Donat's Bay.

**3** Cross the slipway, then climb a flight of steps up the far side of the bay leading to more sycamore and beech woods. When the trees end, continue on the path between arable fields and the cliff edge. *This section can become overgrown with grass and hedge in high summer. Ahead, the white beacon of Nash Point Lighthouse rears up across the fields.* As you approach the lighthouse, the path becomes more open until a final patch of rough grass leads to the complex itself. Pass by the working lighthouse and then a sequence of white buildings, including some enormous foghorns. *Some of these cottages are now holiday lets and there is also a visitor centre in the final building. The geographical significance of Nash Point is not evident on the ground – no dramatic headland protrudes far into the sea. However, it is here that the coast of southern Wales turns from a westerly to a north-westerly direction*

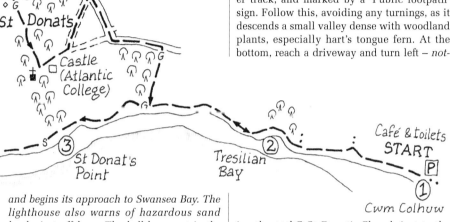

the wall down towards the buildings at Park Farm. The path passes to the left of the buildings before reaching a lane. Turn right, following the lane past the farm for a few yards, until the lane turns sharply back to the left.

**6** At this junction, leave the lane and keep straight ahead, through a gate into the woods, marked with a public bridleway sign. Go through another gate and begin descending. In about 100 yards, watch very carefully for a left hand fork, leaving the broader track, and marked by a 'Public footpath' sign. Follow this, avoiding any turnings, as it descends a small valley dense with woodland plants, especially hart's tongue fern. At the bottom, reach a driveway and turn left – not-

*and begins its approach to Swansea Bay. The lighthouse also warns of hazardous sand banks just offshore. The bell buoy out in the water, easily mistaken for a church bell, gives a similar warning.* From the lighthouse complex follow the tarmac access road a short distance to the car parking area and refreshment cabin at Nash Point.

**4** Leave the Coast path here and continue along the approach lane to the village of Marcross, about ¾ mile inland. *The Fox and Hounds offers refreshments here.*

**5** In Marcross village, turn right to follow the road towards Llantwit Major. In less than ¼ mile, soon after the last houses, turn right down a 'No through road'. When the tarmac ends, go through a gate next to a bungalow and keep straight ahead, the farm to your right. Just before the next gate, and opposite the farm, turn left over a stile, cross a short field to a further stile, then pass diagonally across a larger arable field. At the far side, cross another stile, then turn left to follow

ing the 11thC St Donat's Church just to the right. The driveway climbs amidst sycamore trees with St Donat's Castle high up to the right. Reaching the car park and entrance to Atlantic College in St Donat's Castle, turn left, continuing to follow the driveway, marked as a 'No through road'. Follow this to the gates at the main entrance of the college. Turn right to walk along the road. In 300 yards, follow the road as it turns sharply to the left by another entrance to Atlantic College. In another 300 yards, where the big boundary wall ends, turn right through a kissing gate into King George's Field. It's just a short way to the Coast Path. Turn left here and follow the path back to Cwm Colhuw.

**Wales Coast Path: Stage 6**
**Cwm Colhuw to Nash Point**
This walk follows the Coast Path from the start to Point 4 just past Nash Point. To continue to follow it towards Ogmore, jump from Point 4 to the start of Walk 7.

## WALK 7

# NASH POINT & CWM NASH

**DESCRIPTION** The cliffs along the Glamorgan Heritage Coast consist of layers of shale and limestone. The strata are clearly visible in the profile of the face. This geology makes the coastline both dramatic and unstable. Erosion of the cliffs has produced a 'shore platform' of rock and shingle that extends seawards from the base of the cliffs. Hidden sandbanks have also evolved a little way out in the Channel. Nearby Nash Point lighthouse was built in 1832 to protect shipping from sandbanks at this point on the coast. The area is also a site of special scientific interest, particularly for grass and plant species.

This route explores the mile of coast north west from Nash Point and the wooded nature reserve at Cwm Nash. The circuit continues through the monastic remains at Monknash and the fields around Broughton and Marcross.

**DISTANCE & TERRAIN** 4½ miles. A linear walk from Nash Point to Cwm Nash and back is about 2½ miles. The coast path is clear with a steep fall and rise at the beginning and another steep descent into Cwm Nash. There is some road walking to link field paths, which cross pasture rather than arable land. The traditional Glamorgan stone stiles are a heritage feature but require a high 'leg over'! There is a pub at Marcross and a small, seasonal refreshment kiosk at Nash Point car park.

**START** Car park at Nash Point, Marcross. Parking charge. Post code: CF61 1ZH. Grid ref: SS 916683. The walk could be started at Marcross village through there is no designated parking area.

**DIRECTIONS** Marcross village is about 4 miles west of Llantwit Major on a minor road past St Donat's. To reach Nash Point, turn down the side road by the Horseshoe pub in Marcross village. It becomes a private road and there is a parking charge at the end. A bus service runs between Llantwit Major and Bridgend via Marcross.

**1** A broad path descends from the kiosk and information board, slanting down into a small valley. At the bottom, turn left and cross a wooden footbridge over Marcross Brook. Climb up the opposite side of the valley by way of a small cleft in the hillside. Cross a rather high and difficult stone stile at the top and then continue along the cliff top on the edge of a field. *The Glamorgan Heritage Coast stretches ahead towards Porthcawl, while inland the view lies across arable fields to the village of Marcross. The cliffs here are vertiginous and loose, so avoid the edge!* After about a mile, drop down steeply to the cove at Cwm Nash. (To continue on the Coast Path, see note below.)

**2** Turn inland to follow the path through Cwm Nash. A pleasant, stone path leads through the shaded, sylvan retreat of Cwm Nash Nature Reserve. At the far end the path ends at a narrow lane. Turn left, then immediately right to follow a footpath beside the stream. In a short distance cross the wooden footbridge on the left and continue ahead on the other side of the water. The route then continues across a series of enclosures separated by stiles. In the fourth field the path drops back down to the water and fords the stream. Beyond this continue alongside the water amidst various earthworks and old ruins, the remains of a monastic grange, or farm. A final stile leads to a road junction. (If you want to shorten the walk here you could turn left and follow the road for a mile to Marcross.)

**3** Keep straight ahead, following the road through the village of Broughton. At the end of the houses, the main road bears left towards Wick. Instead of following this round the bend, keep straight ahead on a minor road for about half a mile. Just after some farm buildings on the right, turn right over a stone stile. Follow the right hand edge of the next couple of large fields, before a smaller field leads to a lane.

**4** Turn right, following the road for ½ mile to Marcross. Continue ahead at the cross roads and follow the lane towards the coast, passing the Horseshoe pub and the church

14

on your right. In ½ mile the lane becomes a private road and leads to the car park at Nash Point.

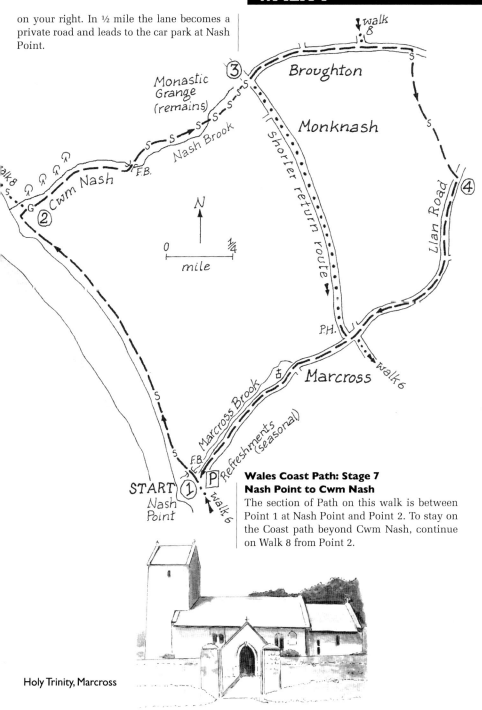

**Wales Coast Path: Stage 7**
**Nash Point to Cwm Nash**
The section of Path on this walk is between Point 1 at Nash Point and Point 2. To stay on the Coast path beyond Cwm Nash, continue on Walk 8 from Point 2.

Holy Trinity, Marcross

## WALK 8

# CWM NASH & CWM BACH

**DESCRIPTION** A Starting from the inland village of Wick, the walk uses two small valleys to connect with the Coast Path. This makes a journey along the cliff top from Cwm Nash to Cwm Bach, above the wide beach of Traeth Mawr and the dramatic face of Whitmore Stairs.

**DISTANCE & TERRAIN** 5 miles. The walk follows pleasant field paths, a wooded cwm and the cliff top. The Coast Path section follows a clear, cliff top route and is largely level except for a climb out of Cwm Nash and a short descent to Cwm Bach. Some stone stiles require reasonably flexible leg joints! There are pubs at Wick and Monknash

**START** Wick village green Post code: CF71 7QE. Grid ref: SS 923722 There is roadside parking available in the village.

**DIRECTIONS** Wick is on the B4265 between Llantwit Major and Bridgend. A bus service runs between these two towns via Wick.

**1** Wick is built around a large triangular village green. Follow Church Street going east towards the church. Opposite the church, turn right, taking a public footpath at the side of the school. Where this ends, a stile leads onto a field, near the remains of a windmill. Continue in a straight line across a series of fields, linked by stone and wooden stiles – *soon enjoying views across the Bristol Channel and across to Somerset and Devon.* In the field with stables and a paddock, the stile can be found in the far left corner. Cross an arable field, then a patch of rough ground to pass between two houses. At the lane, turn right and continue into Broughton. On entering the village, keep straight ahead along Water Street, passing a series of houses and come to a T-junction as you enter the adjacent village of Monknash.

**2** On the opposite side of the junction, cross a stile. Take the right of way across a series of small fields. *There are various earthworks and old ruins here, the remains of* a monastic grange, or farm. After the fourth stile, ford the small stream on your right and then veer left to follow above the bank. The first stile is at the end of the top edge of this field and the route then continues across a sequence of enclosures. In about ¼ mile, watch out for a wooden footbridge on the left hand side of the field. Cross this and then turn right to follow the opposite bank of the stream, leading to a stile onto a narrow lane. Turn left and then immediately right to take the public footpath through Blaen-y-Cwm Nature reserve. A pleasant, stone path leads back down to the sea.

**3** Join the Coast path, crossing the concrete footbridge to the right and going through the gate above. Immediately, double back to follow a narrow, but clear grassy footpath climbing diagonally. *Once at the top, pause for breath and continue along the tops with the dramatic cliffs at Whitmore Stairs now looming ahead. Just before arriving above the cleft at Cwm Bach, you pass the ditch and ramparts of an Iron Age fort.* Although Cwm Bach is, as its name suggests, quite small, it compensates for size with gradient. Don't go straight down into the cleft. Instead, follow the route of the Coast Path which turns inland here. Go through a gate and follow a track for about 200 yards. Then turn left through another gate and descend to the bottom of the valley. (To continue with the Coast Path leave the circular walk here and see note below.)

**4** Otherwise, turn right at the bottom of Cwm Bach, crossing a stile into an area of rough grassland. A narrow path, but mostly evident on the ground, makes its way through the rough grassland and crosses a couple more fields. It maintains a straight course, eventually reaching a stile into a narrow hedged lane. This may be a bit overgrown, so have a stick ready, but it's only just over 200 yards to the road.

*(see map - Coast)*

*Trwyn y Witch*

**5** Turn right and take the road for about ¼ mile. Just after a side turning to the right, turn left into Monk's Wood, an open access area. Go through a gate, keeping to the right hand side of the clearing to find a stile in the far corner. Continue across the next few fields linked by stiles before a greenway between two buildings leads to the road on the edge of Wick village. Turn left to find the village green a few yards away.

of room to walk. *Ahead lies the village of Southerndown and further on, in the distance, you can see Porthcawl and the Gower extending into the sea.*

At the end of the open cliff, the cleft of Cwm Mawr lies below. The Coast Path makes a loop in and around this. It descends diago-

nally down into the wooded Cwm Mawr. At the bottom of the shaded recess, cross a footbridge. The path then reverses direction and climbs the opposite bank diagonally, to regain the top of the cliff. Continue along the cliff top, looking ahead to the remains of the fort on the headland of Trwyn y Witch. Another gate takes the path gently downhill to Cwm y Buarth. Keep straight on the tarmac track, past the walled gardens and down to the car park at Dunraven Bay.

*The Glamorgan Coast Heritage Centre is a short way up a road to the right. There are also toilets here.* Continue up a flight of steps next to the road soon arriving at a car park on the cliff top.

### Wales Coast Path: Stage 8
### Cwm Nash to Dunraven Bay

This walk follows the Coast path from Point 3 at Cwm Nash to Point 4 at Cwm Bach. To continue on the Path from the bottom of Cwm Bach, climb the opposite side, with the wall to the right. At the top, go through a gate, turn left and follow the coast path along the edge of the field. Another gate soon leads to the open cliff top. Follow this for about ¼ mile, taking care, because the cliff is loose and unfenced, though there's plenty

# WALK 9

# OGMORE-BY-SEA

**DESCRIPTION** Ogmore-by-Sea (Aberogwr) lies at the point where the Ogwr estuary meets the sea. The grass and bracken covered hills around Ogmore Down are a fine complement to the dramatic sea cliffs of Southerndown and Dunraven. The sands on this stretch of coast are the most extensive west of Barry.

This walk is in four sections: an initial cliff top and seashore promenade along the coast; a path along the estuary; an ascent through Ogmore Down; and field paths and woods to return to the coast. A varied and satisfying circuit.

**DISTANCE & TERRAIN** 6 miles along cliff and field paths, with short sections of road walking. One long and one short climb. There are pubs and shops near to the walk in St Bride's and in Ogmore-by-Sea. There is also a seasonal kiosk at Dunraven Bay. Toilets available in the car parks at Ogmore-by-Sea and Dunraven Bay.

**START** Dunraven Bay car park (charge). Post code: CF32 0RP. Grid ref: SS 885732. There is an alternative car park at the top of the hill leading into Dunraven Bay. The walk could also be started in Ogmore-by-Sea car park (Point 2) or at a small off road parking on the north side of the road near point 3.

**DIRECTIONS** To reach Dunraven Bay follow a side road from Southerndown, which is on the B4524 between Ogmore-by-Sea and St Bride's Major. There is a bus service between Bridgend and Barry which operates through Southerndown, Ogmore-by-Sea and St Bride's Major.

**I** From the car park, climb the hill away from the beach. Use the steps near the refreshment cabin which leads to a path alongside the road. At the top of the hill, just past a cattle grid, find a car park on the left hand side of the road. Go through the gate in the far corner of the car park and follow the path across the grassy cliff top for about ½ mile. Keep to the seaward side of the Barn at West Farm. Pass the grass parking area and continue along the edge of the slope down to the sea, just outside a retaining wall. Care is needed all the way along here, because there are steep drops. Where the retaining wall ends, the path veers right, to deviate around a small dry valley, before continuing downhill towards the sea. It passes along a grassy promenade just above the seashore and below the bracken and gorse clad slopes. The route by-passes the village of Ogmore-by-Sea but its buildings crown the skyline at the top of the bank. Around two miles from the start go through a gate into the extensive seafront car park.

**2** Keep to the lower side of the car park and walk through to the far end, beginning to turn the corner into the Ogwr estuary. At the very end, pick up the Coast Path, which follows a route through bracken between the estuary below and the road above. Later it widens and continues just above the buildings at Portobello House. Continue on a track past a small parking area and up to the road. Turn left and walk alongside the road for 200 yards. (To continue on the Coast Path towards Candleston and Merthyr Mawr keep on the roadside here and see the notes below.)

**3** To continue with this circular walk, turn right to follow a broad bridleway heading towards the bracken-clad downs. It gradually and steadily climbs a small valley, Pant y Cwteri. Part of the way up, pass a stone well on the side of the path. *The yellow and purple of tormentil and thyme add colour to the sandy heathland.* Avoid turnings to the right and keep climbing until you reach the hamlet and common land at Heol-y-Mynydd.

**4** Turn left to go along a strip of common land next to a small road. Follow the road for about ½ mile to the outskirts of St Bride's Major. Join the main road coming in from the right and continue along this for about 200 yards to a junction by a war memorial and the village green. Turn right, passing a reedy pond on the right.

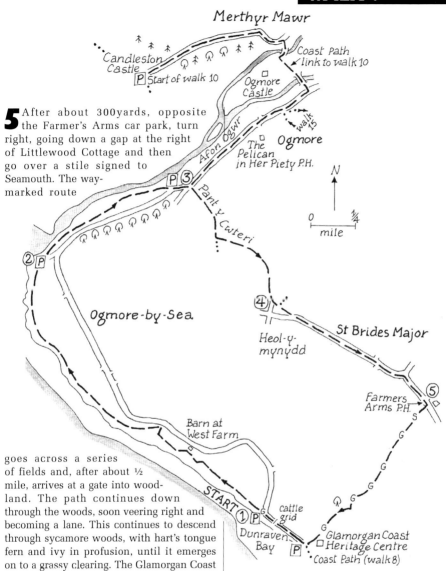

Merthyr Mawr

**5** After about 300yards, opposite the Farmer's Arms car park, turn right, going down a gap at the right of Littlewood Cottage and then go over a stile signed to Seamouth. The way-marked route

goes across a series of fields and, after about ½ mile, arrives at a gate into wood-land. The path continues down through the woods, soon veering right and becoming a lane. This continues to descend through sycamore woods, with hart's tongue fern and ivy in profusion, until it emerges on to a grassy clearing. The Glamorgan Coast Heritage Centre is on the left and, beyond this, a car park, toilets and the sea shore.

### Wales Coast Path: Stage 9
### Dunraven Bay to Candleston Castle
This route follows the Coast Path from Point 1 at Dunraven Bay to Point 3 the bottom of Pant y Cwteri. To stick with the Path, leave this walk at Point 3 and continue along the road to Ogmore village. About ¼

mile after the village pub 'The Pelican in Her Piety', take a footpath to the left and aim for a suspension bridge at the bottom of the field. Cross the bridge to the village of Merthyr Mawr. Turn left and follow the country lane for about ¾ mile to the car park at Candleston Castle. Total distance from point 3 is about 2 miles. Walk 10 and the next section of Coast Path start from here.

19

# MERTHYR MAWR

**DESCRIPTION** Merthyr Mawr is the highest part of the most extensive dune system in Wales. Inland from the coastline the dunes have accumulated on top of a limestone ridge, giving them extra height. Mature trees have colonised the sandy hill while water collects in marshy hollows at the bottom of the dunes.

The walk crosses the dunes to meet the estuary of the River Ogwr. It follows around the coast towards the outskirts of Porthcawl. The return route climbs around the inland flank of the dune system, climbing through extensive woodland.

**DISTANCE & TERRAIN** 5 miles. Until Point 3 the route is on sandy paths, beach and foreshore. Beyond, there is a short urban section before woodland paths. Some gentle climbs. Toilets at the start

**START** Candleston Castle Car Park (pay and display) near Merthyr Mawr village. Post code: CF32 0LS. Grid ref: SS 872773

**DIRECTIONS** Candleston Castle is reached by a minor road through Merthyr Mawr from the A48 Bridgend bypass. There is no public transport to the start.

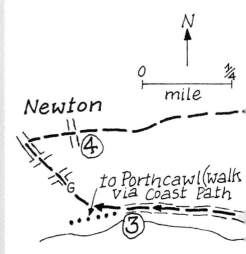

**I** The map shows the link from Walk 9 to the start of this walk at Candleston Castle; directions are included in a footnote to Walk 9. The first part of the walk continues on the Wales Coast Path. At the end of the car park, near the toilets, find a sandy path going into the woods. Soon the path comes out of the trees and crosses the dunes. These are huge, mature dunes and the path itself follows a route through soft sand so it's quite hard work. There are occasional way-marks confirming the course. About ¾ mile after the start, the path arrives at the foreshore and salt marsh. Follow the edge of the dunes and the flat salt marsh area. *Many plants, including evening primrose and thyme colonise the sand.* An information board marks the turning point at the mouth of the Ogwr and the border with the sea. If it's clear you can see across to Devon.

**2** Turn right here and follow the coast line towards Porthcawl, walking along the broad expanse of beach for about a mile. On approaching a rocky section of foreshore, the path regains the dunes and follows a course along the edge of the dunes, just outside the boundary of the nature reserve. Keep on this course for about a mile, ignoring any side turnings. Just after another information board, with the houses of Porthcawl not far ahead, the path forks. (To continue on the Coast Path see note below.)

**3** To continue with this circular, leave the Coast Path here and take a slight right fork. A clear gravel path then leads through the dunes to the edge of a housing estate. Continue towards the end of the cul-de-sac, cross the road and continue on the path on the opposite side through the built-up area. Cross another road and continue straight ahead for just over 100 yards, looking out for a footpath sign on the right hand side of the road. Turn right here and follow the tarmac path between the houses. Continue ahead over one final residential road.

**4** The route opposite now becomes more like a real footpath and returns to the countryside through bracken and later woodland. The path climbs almost imperceptibly. After a while the height gained affords some glimpses across the sea. At a T junction

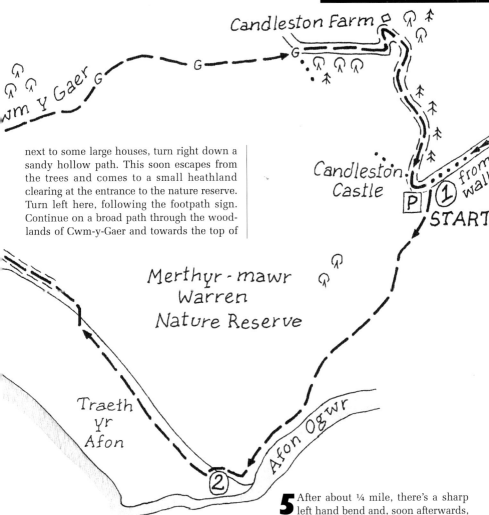

Candleston Farm

Cwm y Gaer

Candleston Castle

P ① from walk 9

START

Merthyr - mawr Warren Nature Reserve

Traeth yr Afon

Afon Ogwr

②

next to some large houses, turn right down a sandy hollow path. This soon escapes from the trees and comes to a small heathland clearing at the entrance to the nature reserve. Turn left here, following the footpath sign. Continue on a broad path through the woodlands of Cwm-y-Gaer and towards the top of a small valley. Pass through a gate. *The enormous scale of the dunes is clearly apparent with huge mountains of sand towering above the path. So well-established are these dunes that mature trees cap the summits.* Keep on the sandy path. At a fork, keep right and continue steadily uphill, weaving through trees and ferns for about ¾ mile. At the gateway out of the nature reserve, keep left and emerge onto a vehicle track. Follow this to the right.

**5** After about ¼ mile, there's a sharp left hand bend and, soon afterwards, a right hand turn as the track approaches Candleston Farm. On the inside of this bend, turn sharp right to follow another track down a small valley. This reaches the car park and start in just under ½ mile.

**Wales Coast Path: Stage 10**
**Candleston Castle to Porthcawl Harbour**
To stay with the Coast Path, follow this walk as far as Point 3. Then, instead of turning inland, keep left follow the coast around the holiday parks and buildings of Porthcawl. Continue past Newton Point, Trecco Bay and Sandy Bay to reach the town and its harbour.

# PORTHCAWL & REST BAY

**DESCRIPTION** At the beginning of the twentieth century, Porthcawl was a place for convalescence. The bracing air was believed to be a good remedy for TB and other respiratory illnesses acquired in the industrial valleys of south Wales. The town centre is unremarkable with the usual small town chain store names. But its atmosphere is almost intimate. The whole of southern Wales mingles here, as if the egalitarian spirit of nonconformity has spilled out of the valleys to colonise the coast. The promenade is over a mile long and offers fantastic views along the coast and across to the hills of Exmoor, clearly visible on a reasonable day.

The walk follows the seafront and shore for two miles, with an optional extension beyond to Sker Point or even Kenfig. You may prefer simply to retrace your steps. But an inland circuit is offered in the interest of variety.

**DISTANCE & TERRAIN** 6 miles. Promenade and field paths with a section of suburban road on the return. There are plenty of cafes and shops in Porthcawl. Toilets at Rest Bay and in the town centre

**START** Porthcawl Harbour. Post code: CF31 4AP. Grid ref:.SS 819764.

**DIRECTIONS** The walk starts from close to the centre of Porthcawl. The town is easily reached by the A4229 from Junction 37 on the M4. There are regular buses from Bridgend and Port Talbot. The nearest station is Pyle (about 4 miles).

**I** From the harbour, walk along the esplanade – *soon passing the Grand Pavilion, built in 1932. The esplanade itself was built to commemorate Queen Victoria's Jubilee in 1887.* In about ¾ mile, you come to a shelter and information board marking the beginning of Lock's Common. The official Coast Path, for some reason, keeps straight on here to follow the road and cycle path. However, a preferable route is to turn left here and follow the footpath around the open common, next to the rocky shore. *Lock's Common is protect-* ed as a nature reserve because of the heathland habitat and some sections of karst (limestone pavement). The.path returns to the road by the lifeguard station at Rest Bay.

**2** At the far side of the building, walk across the last section of common and find a concrete track. Follow this through a gate and continue along a wooden walkway. The boardwalk continues along the edge of Rest Bay between the sea and a golf course. *Oystercatchers and herring gulls forage for food on the intertidal sands, while dune plants colonise the foreshore.* The boardwalk ends at a gate.

**3** *To explore Sker Point, continue straight ahead through a gate to cross an open area of grass land, dotted with thyme and wild flowers. Follow the coast path across this area for about ½ mile and come to a crossing of tracks by a grassy headland that divides Rest Bay from Sker Beach and Kenfig Sands. When you're ready, return to Point 3. This adds about 1 mile to the walk. (It is also possible to continue beyond Sker Point to Kenfig Nature Reserve (see Walk 17).* You could return directly along the outward route, but for a circuit, turn inland at Point 3. Follow a footpath between the golf course and a series of fields. In about a mile, go through a gate to reach a road.

**4** Turn right, walk along the pavement at the side of the road into the outskirts of Porthcawl. The bus service between Porthcawl and Kenfig follows this road. In about ½ mile turn right into Anglesey Way. Follow the road through the housing estate for ¼ mile. *Relieve any monotony by guessing which Welsh island comes next (all roads on this estate are named after islands off the Welsh coast).* Just after passing Grassholm Close (on the right), watch out for a public footpath sign, also to the right. Take the pleasant hedge-lined route between the built-up area and the fields, leading to the common land at Rest Bay. From the lifeguard

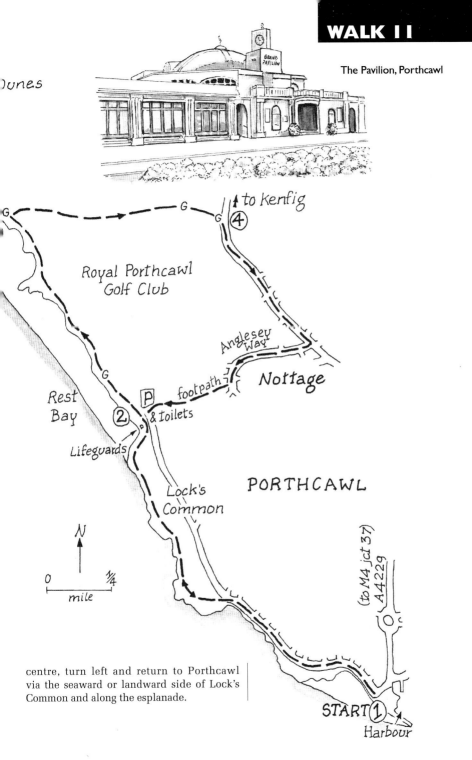

The Pavilion, Porthcawl

)unes

G ← → G G ↑ to Kenfig ④

Royal Porthcawl
Golf Club

Anglesey Way

G

footpath Nottage

Rest
Bay

P

② & toilets

Lifeguards

Lock's
Common

PORTHCAWL

N

0 ¼
mile

(to M4 jct 37)
A4229

centre, turn left and return to Porthcawl
via the seaward or landward side of Lock's
Common and along the esplanade.

START ①
Harbour

# PORTHKERRY & COLD KNAP

**DESCRIPTION** Porthkerry Country Park straddles a small valley, just inland from the great bulk of Bull Cliff. It provides a public area of broad open grassland, woods and cliffs. This walk follows a figure of eight around the area; though the eastern loop is longer than the western. You can of course do one or the other or both.

The eastern loop climbs through Cliff Woods and circles round the pebble beach, headland and harbour at Cold Knap, the quieter end of Barry. It returns through Romiley Park and the woodland fringe of Porthkerry Country Park itself. Be aware that Romiley Park itself is locked at dusk. The western loop is a short excursion up into the historic village of Porthkerry

## DISTANCE & TERRAIN

Eastern loop 2½ miles; western loop 1 mile. The route follows cliff and woodland paths and tracks. There is one section of promenade and another through a park. There is a short, steep climb on both loops. There is a café next to the main car park at the start of the walk. There are toilets here and at other places on the route.

## START

Main car park, Porthkerry Country Park, Barry. Postcode: CF62 3ZP. Grid ref: ST 085669. Car park charge at weekends and bank holidays.

## DIRECTIONS

Porthkerry Country Park is on the eastern fringe of Barry and is signposted from main roads into the town. A regular bus service from Barry centre, Penarth and Cardiff serves point 3.

### EASTERN LOOP

**1** From the car park follow the tarmac path towards the sea. *It passes just to the right of woodland, near the site of a medieval corn mill.* Just before the raised pebble beach, the path veers left, curving round to the foot of a flight of concrete steps, the 'Golden Stairs'. Climb these into Cliff Woods, a local nature reserve, and follow the path along the edge of steep limestone cliffs. *Through the thick*

*vegetation there are glimpses of the Bristol Channel and the coast of Somerset. When the path leaves the wood, continue to walk along the edge of the mowed green sward, now with spectacular views. Drop steeply down the grass bank and continue on the path between some bushes to land on the sea front. On the left pass the remains*

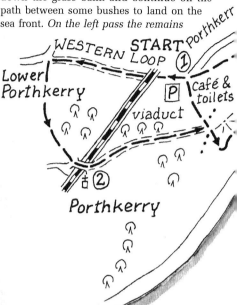

*of some Roman remains. Their purpose is unknown but educated speculation suggests they may have been public buildings connected with their coastal location. There are also toilets at this point.*

**2** Keep straight along the promenade next to the raised pebble beach. At the end, the tarmac path turns left, but first detour to circle round the grassy headland at Cold Knap Point. Back on the main path, pass the dilapidated lifeguard building, then head north past Watch House Bay and the entrance to the old Barry Harbour. The present docks are further east, on the other side of the town. At the end of the little bay, follow the road as it turns left rather than keeping straight ahead on the Wales Coast Path. The road, Lake Side, effectively loops around the park, with flats and houses on the right and the ornamental lake and park on the left. At a road junction keep straight ahead and soon pass under a railway arch.

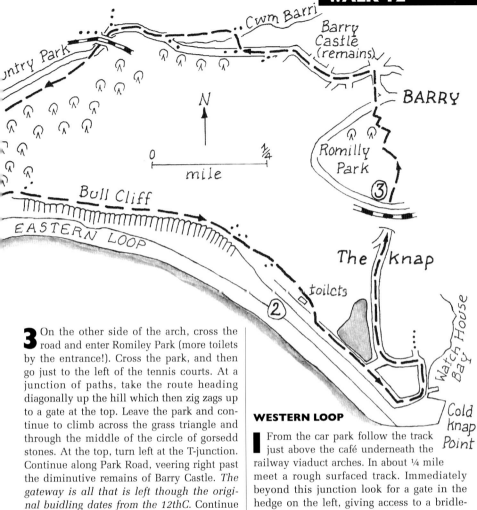

**3** On the other side of the arch, cross the road and enter Romiley Park (more toilets by the entrance!). Cross the park, and then go just to the left of the tennis courts. At a junction of paths, take the route heading diagonally up the hill which then zig zags up to a gate at the top. Leave the park and continue to climb across the grass triangle and through the middle of the circle of gorsedd stones. At the top, turn left at the T-junction. Continue along Park Road, veering right past the diminutive remains of Barry Castle. *The gateway is all that is left though the original buidling dates from the 12thC.* Continue over the brow of the hill and on down the entrance drive to Porthkerry Country Park. In about 200 yards, watch out for a flight of steps between railings on the right. These are easy to miss and begin just next to a ramp on the road. Go down the steps into Cwm Barri. Cross the footbridge and then turn left to follow the path. This continues through a grassy clearing, to meet the driveway again. Continue ahead, past a small car park and under a railway bridge. Beyond the bridge a wide open grassy area opens out. Walk across this, just below the driveway, and along the wooded fringes of the park, back to the start point.

## WESTERN LOOP

**1** From the car park follow the track just above the café underneath the railway viaduct arches. In about ¼ mile meet a rough surfaced track. Immediately beyond this junction look for a gate in the hedge on the left, giving access to a bridleway. Follow the route alongside the hedge with views back to the viaduct. Then climb up the path through woodland, emerging at the top by a farm and village green. *Porthkerry church is at the far end of the green.*

**2** Turn left in front of the church, following the left of the two driveways, signed 'Public footpath to the beach'. The footpath leaves the driveway at a gateway to a property and continues downhill through the trees. At the bottom, arrive at a pitch and putt course. Negotiate your way round the edge of this back to the start.

## WALK 13

# CWM COLHUW

**DESCRIPTION** Llantwit Major became one of the most significant centres of Celtic Christianity, following the foundation of a church and college here by St Illtud in about 508 AD. It is now a sizeable community, merging into neighbouring Boverton and close to the military base at St Athan. However, the centre retains a warren of narrow streets weaving between stone buildings. The town is in the heart of the Vale of Glamorgan, lying about a mile inland from the coast. The landscape between Llantwit Major and the sea, which this walk explores, is a mixture of limestone scrub and grassland culminating in the distinctive shale and limestone cliffs of the Heritage Coast. Much of Cwm Colhuw is a nature reserve. Although a relatively short walk, there is enormous variety here, including limestone grassland, cliffs, beach and woodland, as well as some of Llantwit Major's appealing townscape.

**DISTANCE & TERRAIN** 2½ miles, including paths, tracks and grassland with short sections of lane walking. Some short climbs. All facilities in Llantwit Major.

**START** Car park next to the Town Hall, Burial Lane, Llantwit Major. Post code: CF61 1SD. Grid ref: SS 967687.

**DIRECTIONS** Llantwit Major is easily reached by road from Barry, Cowbridge and Bridgend. There is an hourly train service from Cardiff and Bridgend on the Vale of Glamorgan line. The station is a short walk from the Town Hall. There is also a regular bus service between Barry and Bridgend via Llantwit.

**❚** *The distinctive and curious Town Hall has been home to the community council and its predecessors since the end of the nineteenth century, but its pedigree stretches back to Norman times when it was a courthouse. As well as offices it hosts an information and heritage centre.* Walk to the far side of the building and follow Burial Lane, a narrow road which goes downhill to the left. Pass the parish church – *dedicated to St Illtud who founded a church here in about 500 AD on an earlier Celtic holy site. The*

*present building dates from the Norman period.* Where the lane turns sharp right to become Church Street, keep straight ahead up some steps. At the top, turn left along a drive way. Almost immediately, cross a stone stile to the right into a field, crowned by an old dovecot. Take the left of the two field paths, running almost parallel to the drive. Climb another stile and carry on down another patch of land to reach a farm track, leading to a road. Follow the road to the right, later becoming a track.

**2** Soon the track bends round to the right and passes between a variety of barns, climbing up to contour the rim of Cwm Colhuw through limestone country. . When the track veers right into a field, keep straight ahead along a green lane between hedgerows. As it approaches the cliff top the path bursts out of the shrubbery to reveal a wide panorama, stretching from the shale and limestone cliffs of St Donat's Point to the stone shelf and beach on the shore at Cwm Colhuw. Turn left to join the Coast Path, down the steps to reach the beach. *Facilities here include a café, toilets, car park and lifeguard station. There is evidence that there may have been a Roman harbour here.*

**3** Cross to the far side of the cwm and climb the steps on the far side. At the top go past a gate/stile and then leave the Coast Path, instead bearing left to follow a path along the side of open heath land. *This open area is part of Castle Ditches, a Celtic fort dating back 2,700 years. It is one of a number of Iron Age forts along the coast; there are others at Summerhouse Bay (Walk 5) and Nash Point (Walks 6 and 7).* Pass through an area of shrubs and hedges to reach a double gate/stile. You can follow either route here, but it's probably easier to take the right hand option, passing an information panel and walking across a large open paddock. At the far end of the field cross another stile and

walk
6

cafe & toil

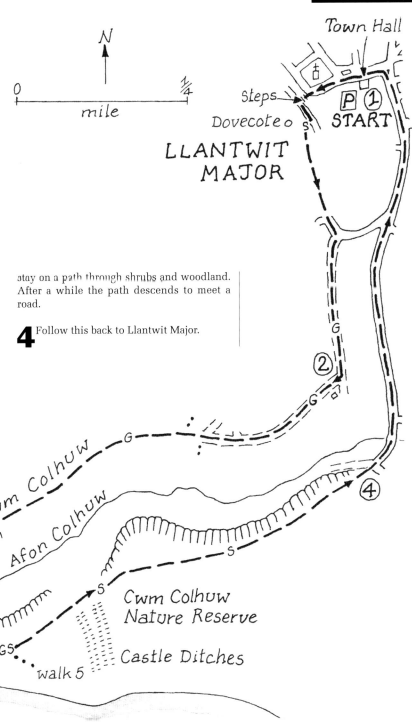

*Town Hall*

Steps

Dovecote o

**START**

**LLANTWIT MAJOR**

N

0 | mile | ¼

stay on a path through shrubs and woodland. After a while the path descends to meet a road.

**4** Follow this back to Llantwit Major.

Cwm Colhuw

Afon Colhuw

**Cwm Colhuw Nature Reserve**

**Castle Ditches**

walk 5

27

# DUNRAVEN

**DESCRIPTION** Dunraven Bay is also known as Southerndown Beach. Its combination of sand and shingle, embraced by the steep cliffs of Witch's Point, make it an appealing and atmospheric destination, so it can be very busy in summer. The headland of Witch's Point (Trwyn y Witch) is a great place to explore. The ruins of an early 19thC mansion, known as Dunraven Castle lie half way up. The residence was demolished in 1963 and lies on the site of a number of earlier mansions. Lower down, the walled gardens are still open to the public during daylight. You can also visit the Glamorgan Heritage Coast Centre, a short way up a lane from the beach. This is a short walk using permissive paths and the Wales Coast Path to explore the area of Dunraven and the section of coast leading to Cwm Mawr.

**DISTANCE & TERRAIN** 2 miles, an undulating route on tracks and field paths. Toilets and seasonal refreshment cabin in Dunraven Bay car park.

**START** Dunraven Bay car park (charge). Post code: CF32 0RP. Grid ref: SS 885732. There is an alternative car park at the top of the hill leading into Dunraven Bay.

**DIRECTIONS** To reach Dunraven Bay, follow a side road from Southerndown, situated on the B4524 between Ogmore-by-Sea and St Bride's Major. There is a bus service between Bridgend and Barry which operates through Southerndown.

**I** Start from the main car park next to the beach. Leave the car park, passing the lodge and then continue along the tarmac driveway out of Dunraven Bay. Ignore the left hand turning to the upper car park and keep on straight ahead towards the woods and the ruins of the castle. In about 300 yards, just before the walled gardens, turn left off the main concrete track, to follow a permissive track going inland. (*The Walled Gardens are open to the public during daylight. It's worth making time to look inside either now or at the end of the walk.*) The track follows a shallow valley, between open fields and woodland, to arrive at a rock-castellated gatehouse.

**2** Immediately before the building, turn right, leaving the track to cross a stile. The permissive path goes between the wall and a field. In about ¼ mile, just after the top of the hill, turn right through a gateway, along another permissive path. Shortly, cross a stile and bear left to pick up the start of a grassy track. After about 100 yards, this turns to the right, through another gateway and becomes a stony drive. This descends a shallow valley to Cwm y Buarth. You reach an open grass area just before the cliffs. This is also a junction with the Coast Path.

**3** To extend the walk turn left, and follow the Coast Path for about ¼ mile to reach the cliff top above Cwm Mawr, a deep, wooded indentation in the coastline. *Cwm Mawr is a hanging valley, created by melting glacial water. Upstream the valley is dry but water reappears lower down before dropping into the sea via a waterfall.* The path deviates inland to negotiate the cwm, descending into the wooded recess, crossing the stream by a footbridge. Climb the opposite side to leave the woodland and gain the cliff top.

**4** Enjoy the view across the Heritage Coast. You can of course continue further along the Coast Path if the fancy takes you. If you reach Cwm Bach you link with Walk 8. Otherwise, turn back here and retrace your steps to Point 3 at Cwm y Buarth. At Point 3, turn left at the grass clearing to find a path leading through the woods and around the headland, known as Trwyn y Witch (Witch's Point). Pass an interpretation panel and continue along the path. There are lots of side routes to explore on this headland, but for now keep to the track, as it climbs to the site of Dunraven Castle, crowning the promontory. *This is the site of an Iron Age fort and, later, the Normans built on the headland. However, the present remains are little more than 200 years old.*

28

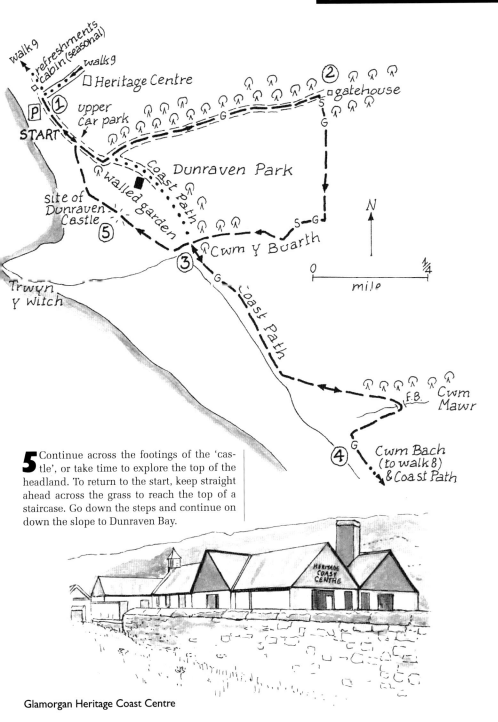

**walk 9**

**refreshments cabin (seasonal)**

**walk 9**

☐ Heritage Centre

② gatehouse

upper car park

Dunraven Park

START

walled garden

Coast Path

site of Dunraven Castle

⑤

Cwm y Buarth

③

Trwyn y Witch

N

0 ¼ mile

Coast Path

Cwm Mawr
F.B.

④ Cwm Bach
(to walk 8)
& Coast Path

**5** Continue across the footings of the 'castle', or take time to explore the top of the headland. To return to the start, keep straight ahead across the grass to reach the top of a staircase. Go down the steps and continue on down the slope to Dunraven Bay.

Glamorgan Heritage Coast Centre

# OGMORE DOWN & COED-Y-BWL

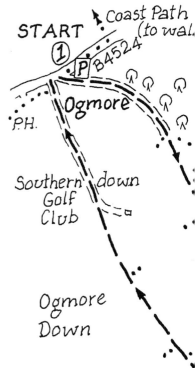

**DESCRIPTION** Ogmore Down is a tract of unenclosed common rising on a wedge of land between the coast and the estuary of the River Ogwr. There are a number of archaeological remains across the Down, and more recently quarries have exploited the carboniferous limestone. The upland area rises from the coast to about 300 feet and the common is used for grazing shared with a golf course. The walk crosses the Down to St Bride's village, then exploring the wooded valley of the Alun and the nature reserve at Coed y Bwl.

**DISTANCE & TERRAIN** 4½ miles. Most of the walk lies along easy grass ribbons through open land. There are some sections of quiet lane and a wooded nature reserve. One significant climb. There is a shop at St Bride's Major and pubs at both Ogmore and at St Bride's. The walk can be shortened by turning back at Points 2 or 3.

**START** Small lay by on the south side of the B4524 on the edge of Ogmore village, about 300 yards east of the 'Pelican in her Piety'. Post code: CF32 0QP. Grid ref:.SS 884768.

**DIRECTIONS** From Bridgend follow the B4265 towards Ewenny and then the B4524 towards Ogmore-by-Sea. Just over a mile from Ewenny, you enter the small village of Ogmore. Just next to the 'Ogmore' sign, there's a lay by. (Note that Ogmore-by-Sea is a different location, another 1½ miles further on.) There is a bus service from Bridgend, which is also the nearest station, about 3 miles away.

Next to the lay by and the Ogmore sign, a narrow tarmac lane leaves the main road, to climb the hillside diagonally. Towards the top, the tarmac ends and the route continues on a flat, stony track onto the open common land of Ogmore Down. When the land opens out and the track ends, keep straight ahead. The common is shared with a golf course and a grassy path leads ahead, just to the left of a green. Maintain a forward course towards the village of St Brides, with houses visible ahead, soon passing along the (fenced) edge of a massive quarry.

**2** At the far end of the common, arrive at a road end and small parking area. Turn left and follow the broad grassy route next to the hedge. The hedge curves round past a house and reaches another tarmac lane. Follow this past some more houses, enjoying views inland across Bridgend to the hills beyond. The lane gradually descends through trees to meet a busy road on the edge of St Bride's Major.

**3** Cross the road and climb the grassy strip opposite. At the top, turn left to follow a track along the edge of the hillside. Pass a couple of houses and then continue along the broad grassy ribbon. Turn sharp right at the corner of the wall and continue, slightly downhill. Keep on the grassy track, ignoring any side turnings and, after about ¾ mile, drop more steeply to go through a gate into the nature reserve at Coed-y-Bwl woods. At the bottom of the hill, leave the woods and come to a quiet road running uphill alongside the waters of the River Alun.

**4** Follow the lane right for just under ½ a mile to a road junction, next to Black Hall Farm. Turn right and follow this lane for another ¾ mile to enter the village of St Bride's Major. Keep on the lane as it veers left and descends into the village, joining a main road.

**5** Turn left and follow the road for a few yards. Opposite the Fox and Hounds pub, turn right, taking a lane towards the church. Follow this past the church and on out of the village. Cross a cattle grid and keep on the tarmac lane as it bears right. Follow this until it ends on the common at Point 2. From here, there are two broad grassy tracks ahead. The right hand fork is the outward route of the walk. Instead, take the left hand fork and follow this grassy clearing across Ogmore Down, keeping a straight line. Later, watch out for golf balls as the course shares the common! Pick up the golf club access track and follow this back down to the main road at the start.

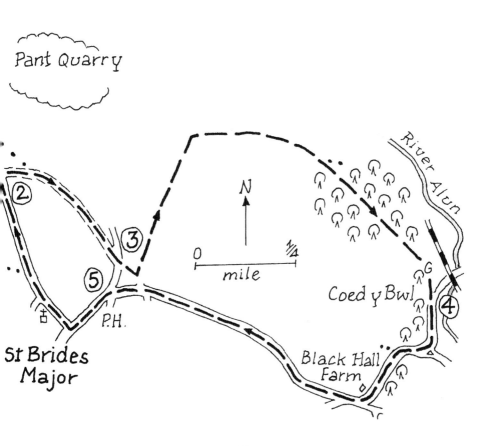

# KENFIG DUNES & NATURE RESERVE

**DESCRIPTION** A vast dune system extends along much of the Glamorgan coast. One of the most extensive areas is at Kenfig. Here the dunes stretch northwards for over 2 miles from the headland at Sker Point towards the industrial landscape of Margam. Inland the sand continues for a similar distance, even reaching a tentacle beyond the M4 towards Pyle. In the centre of the dunes, close to the Visitor Centre is Kenfig Pool, the largest tract of fresh water in Wales, south of Llangorse Lake in the Brecon Beacons.

Both walks start at the Visitor Centre which helps to interpret the ecology of the national nature reserve. There are various waymarked walks from here. **Walk 16** uses one of these as an introduction to the area, offering a circular route to the seashore at Sker Beach. **Walk 17** (3 miles) extends to the rocky headland of Sker Point before tracing a route around the south of the area across heathland.

**DISTANCE & TERRAIN** Walk 16 (2 miles) uses sandy paths through the dunes. Walk 17 (3 miles) also follows heathland tracks but there is no significant climbing. Information and toilets are available at the visitor centre. There is a pub less than ½ mile north along the road from the centre.

**START** Kenfig National Nature Reserve Visitor Centre. There is a car park here. Post code: CF64 3EE. Grid ref: SS 802811.

**DIRECTIONS** The Centre is easily reached by an unclassified road from Porthcawl (3 miles) or Pyle (2 miles). The nearest station is at Pyle.

## WALK 16
## SKER BEACH

This is the Nature Reserve's circular route to Sker Beach and way marked with numbered posts and yellow marks. Follow the path from the back of the centre. In a few yards, turn left at a T-junction, following the sign to

Sker Beach. A broad sandy path leads through bracken. Soon, come to a junction with a permissive bridleway, but ignore this, keeping on the sandy path, signed to the beach, and still following numbered yellow way marks. Glimpses across the vast dune system emphasise the huge area covered by a warren of sand hills. *Views extend beyond the steel works at Port Talbot to Swansea Bay and the Gower peninsula.* The path continues to weave through bracken covered dunes towards the sea. Just before the final dunes and the sea, the path reaches a T-junction, with a wide track going left to right. This is the Wales Coast Path, also known as the Haul Road.

**2** Turn right and follow the broad, roughly surfaced track for about ¼ mile. It heads north, just inside the dunes, with distant views up the coast and into the hilly hinterland beyond Port Talbot. The Sker Beach waymarked walk heads inland from post 15, about ¼ mile north of the point where the path reached the beach. (If you want to extend the walk you can keep going north on the Haul Road for 2 miles until it comes to a footbridge across the Afon Cynffig and the beginning of Margam Burrows. You could then return to Point 3 or follow other tracks back to the Centre.)

**3** Otherwise, turn right here, going inland and following the yellow way marks back to the Visitor Centre. The path weaves across sandy dunes and heathland. A short deviation to the left, just before the centre, will bring you to the edge of Kenfig Pool.

## WALK 17
## SKER ROCKS & KENFIG HEATH

**1** Follow the directions for Walk 16 as far as Point 2. The route as far as the beach is waymarked in yellow. Meet the Coast Path at a T-junction.

**2** Turn left and follow the path to the end of Sker Beach, passing a metal cabin here. After a while, pass through a gate and then come to a junction, marked by a post for the Coast Path.

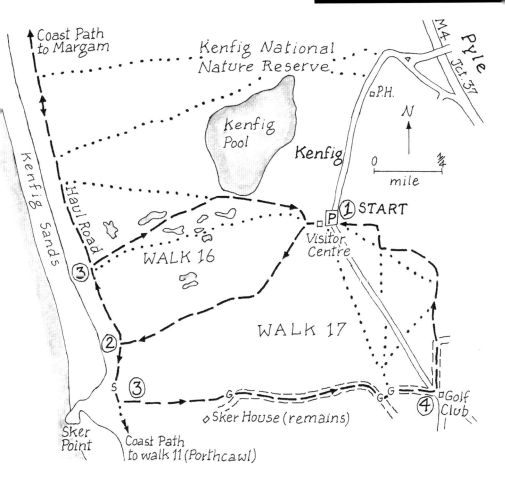

**3** At this point, leave the Coast Path and bear left, going inland on a broad track. Pass a small pond and head towards the yellow painted buildings at Sker House. Keep to the left of the buildings and enclosure of around the house. The track comes to a gate into a farm lane just beyond the buildings. Go through the gate and turn left, following the roughly surfaced lane. In about ½ a mile, leave the track and turn left through a gate, marked as a public footpath. Cross a grass area and reach another gate which leads to a lane beyond. Follow this to the right and it soon arrives at a road opposite the golf club house.

**4** Cross the road and find a tarmac bridleway going half left, to the right of the green. Follow the route gently uphill. Later it becomes roughly surfaced. Just beyond a small chapel, the track turns right into a yard. Leave it here and keep left, taking a grassy path, through bracken, across a tongue of the golf course. Continue alongside a hedge, emerging by some houses and on to a concrete track. Follow the track to the left of the houses. It weaves around to meet the main road opposite the Visitor Centre.

# COWBRIDGE & ST HILARY

**DESCRIPTION** Cowbridge straddles the Roman route between Caerleon and Carmarthen but the town was officially established in 1254 by the Norman Lord of Glamorgan, Richard de Clare. It became an important medieval market town and much of the original walls still stand. Cowbridge also possesses a number of Georgian buildings and has remained an important trading and administrative centre for many centuries.

A walk through the rolling farmland and heath downs in the heart of the Vale of Glamorgan. This inland circuit starts from the attractive and prosperous market town of Cowbridge and passes through the secluded village of St Hilary.

**DISTANCE & TERRAIN** 4 miles. The walk follows an undulating route, mostly along field paths, tracks and lanes. There are all facilities in Cowbridge, including toilets in the car park at the start of the walk.

**START** Cowbridge town centre. There is a large free car park to the rear of the town hall on the north side of the main street. Post code: CF71 7DD. Grid ref: SS 996746.

**DIRECTIONS** Cowbridge lies just off the A48 Cardiff to Bridgend road. Bus X2 runs between Cardiff and Porthcawl via Bridgend and stops by the start of the walk.

I Leave the car park and go through to the main street next to the town hall. Cross the road and turn left along it for about 100 yards, crossing a bridge over the diminutive River Thaw, easily missed. Soon after the bridge, turn right into a small road, 'The Limes', by a signpost to the park. At the end of this small cul-de-sac keep straight ahead along the footpath into the park, with a cemetery to the left and the stream and a supermarket to the right. Opposite a footbridge into a play area, bear left up steps, climbing a small rocky scar into woodland. Continue on this path as it weaves round the back of some houses to reach a lane. Turn right and follow the narrow road, which soon

curves left past the remains of St Quentin's Castle. *This commanded a site oin a loop in the River Thaw and was defended on three sides by this natural moat. A castle was built here during the early years of the Norman Conquest but the present fortification dates from the 14thC. The most impressive ruin is the gatehouse.* Continue along the lane, Castle Hill, until it comes to a T-junction at the bottom of the hill.

2 Turn right, cross the river and in about 100 yards, just after a restored housing complex, turn right to follow a footpath. This starts as a track, then passing some stables and continuing through a series of fields alongside the river. It crosses a footbridge and continues on the other bank, before following water company track to a road.

3 A track continues on the opposite side, just a few yards to the right. But the official right of way keeps straight across a stile opposite, along the bottom of a small field and over another stile to gain the track 100 yards further on. Later the track passes through a cutting in the embankment of an old railway line. After about ¾ mile it ends in front of a private gate into New Beaupre. At this point the path deviates round the property by going left through a gate, up a small paddock, across a stile at the top and then around the top of the grounds through woodland. It emerges onto a tarmac lane at the far side. Continue on up a wooded lane shaded by sycamore and beech trees and with ground cover of ferns, bracken and brambles. The lane soon reaches the village of St Hilary. Continue up the hill and weave through the village, passing a pub on the left and a church to the right.

4 Just after a thatched cottage, reach a small crossroads next to a telegraph pole. Turn left. Follow the tarmac road a short distance before it becomes a green lane between hedgerows. This rises gradually up towards

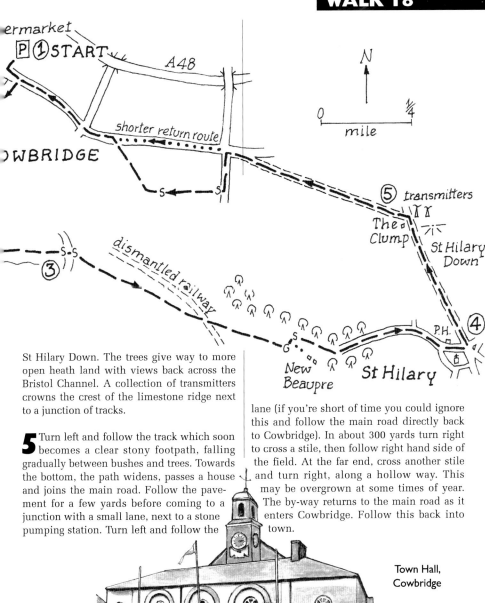

St Hilary Down. The trees give way to more open heath land with views back across the Bristol Channel. A collection of transmitters crowns the crest of the limestone ridge next to a junction of tracks.

**5** Turn left and follow the track which soon becomes a clear stony footpath, falling gradually between bushes and trees. Towards the bottom, the path widens, passes a house and joins the main road. Follow the pavement for a few yards before coming to a junction with a small lane, next to a stone pumping station. Turn left and follow the lane (if you're short of time you could ignore this and follow the main road directly back to Cowbridge). In about 300 yards turn right to cross a stile, then follow right hand side of the field. At the far end, cross another stile and turn right, along a hollow way. This may be overgrown at some times of year. The by-way returns to the main road as it enters Cowbridge. Follow this back into town.

Town Hall, Cowbridge

# LLANDAFF & BUTE PARK

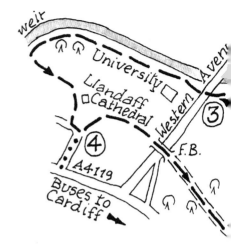

**DESCRIPTION** Cardiff's castle is an iconic representation of the city's history from ancient times through to the Industrial Revolution. Originally the site was a Roman fort guarding the road between Caerleon and Carmarthen as it crossed the Taff. Later the Normans built a castle here. But it was industrial muscle rather than military might that decided its future in the eighteenth century. The first Marquis of Bute bought the castle and converted it into a luxury mansion. The Bute family were responsible for the development of Cardiff as a coal port and were principle architects of the city's Victorian prosperity. Bute Park, only open to the public since 1947, reaches right into the heart of the city. Llandaff Cathedral dates from the 12thC though its position as a place of Christian worship predates this. It lies 2 miles north of Cardiff in a tranquil, historic conservation area overlooking the River Taff.

Starting in the heart of the capital, this is a much more rural and tranquil route than might be expected, crossing Bute Park and then following the River Taff to the historic serenity of Llandaff with its ancient cathedral. There are lots of alternative routes through the park.

**DISTANCE & TERRAIN** 5 miles, flat except for a short climb to Llandaff. The route follows parkland and riverside paths. As well as all the facilities in the centre of Cardiff, there are refreshments available in Llandaff (point 4) and Portcanna (point 5).

**START** West Lodge Gate, Castle Street, Cardiff. Post code: CF10 1BJ. Grid ref: ST 178765.

**DIRECTIONS** The walk starts from the heart of Cardiff, close to all buses and trains. By car, it will be easier to start from Llandaff and walk into the city. There are plenty of buses between the city and Llandaff so it would also be easy to just walk one way. Note: The West Lodge gate into Bute Park closes at dusk, though it is possible to find civilised alternative exits if you get locked in, without scaling castle walls!

**1** Start by Cardiff Castle, opposite the junction of High Street and Castle Street in the city centre. Walk along Castle Street towards the bridge over the River Taff. Just before the bridge, go right through the West Lodge Gate into Bute Park. Soon after the entrance, bear left and take the main path alongside the east bank of the Taff. Pass the summer house and footbridge. Sophia Gardens, home of Glamorgan Cricket Club, is on the opposite bank. Continue along the tarmac track between the river and some walled gardens, then along a small embankment. When the tarmac track veers right away from the river, keep straight ahead on a rougher woodland path following the waterside (though there are plenty of other options).

**2** At the weir, turn left and cross the river on a suspension bridge. On the far bank, turn right and follow the earthen path between a fence and the river through woodland. In about ½ mile, the path curves round to join Western Avenue, a major arterial road across Cardiff, by the park gates.

**3** The route continues on the opposite side of the dual carriageway. To avoid crossing the road directly, use the footbridge about 200 yards west (left) from here. Opposite the park gates, follow the cycleway signposted to Llandaff. It is an earth track, which continues to follow the river upstream alongside the Taff. On the left are the buildings of Cardiff Metropolitan University and soon,

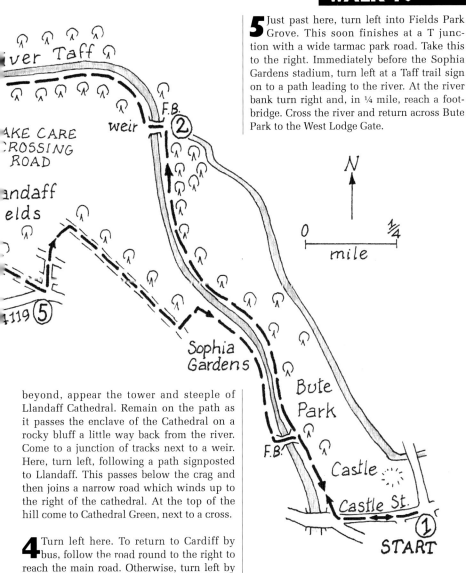

ver Taff

LAKE CARE
CROSSING
ROAD

Llandaff
elds

1119 ⑤

**5** Just past here, turn left into Fields Park Grove. This soon finishes at a T junction with a wide tarmac park road. Take this to the right. Immediately before the Sophia Gardens stadium, turn left at a Taff trail sign on to a path leading to the river. At the river bank turn right and, in ¼ mile, reach a footbridge. Cross the river and return across Bute Park to the West Lodge Gate.

N

0        ¼
mile

weir

F.B.
②

Sophia
Gardens

Bute
Park

F.B.

Castle

Castle St.

①
START

beyond, appear the tower and steeple of Llandaff Cathedral. Remain on the path as it passes the enclave of the Cathedral on a rocky bluff a little way back from the river. Come to a junction of tracks next to a weir. Here, turn left, following a path signposted to Llandaff. This passes below the crag and then joins a narrow road which winds up to the right of the cathedral. At the top of the hill come to Cathedral Green, next to a cross.

**4** Turn left here. To return to Cardiff by bus, follow the road round to the right to reach the main road. Otherwise, turn left by the public toilets, following Cathedral Green downhill past the other side of the cathedral. At the bottom of the hill there is a small car park. Turn right to follow a footpath which goes alongside a playing field to join Western Avenue. Cross the footbridge and continue through the gates into Llandaff Fields. Take the wide tarmac path across the wide open grass field for ½ mile, then arriving at the Cabin Café by the road.

# ST FAGAN'S

**DESCRIPTION** The National History Museum at St Fagan's includes over 40 historic buildings from all over Wales re-erected in a large park. These tell the story of Wales in a unique way, along with a series of indoor galleries. The short walk provided here could be combined with a day out at the museum. Alongside the Museum are extensive formal and cottage gardens surrounding the Tudor castle. The walk is a short circuit along the wooded limestone ridge on which the village of St Fagan's is built, returning alongside the River Ely. The Ely is one of three rivers converging on the capital, along with the Taff and the Rhymney.

**DISTANCE & TERRAIN** 2½ miles. Undulating paths through woods, fields and houses. There is a café at the Museum. Other facilities include toilets and left luggage lockers.

**START** Entrance to St Fagan's National History Museum. Post code: CF5 6XB. Grid ref: ST 117778.

**DIRECTIONS** The Museum is about 5 miles west of the centre of Cardiff and 2 miles from the junction of the A48, A4232 and A4050 at Culverhouse Cross. By public transport reach St Fagan's by bus 32/32A from Cardiff Central Bus Station. Buses take you right to the doors of the museum.

**I** Walk back down the drive past the entrance to the museum and then continue left along the approach lane. There is a wide verge on the right hand side, next to the River Ely. The approach road finishes at a junction near a level crossing. Turn left here and immediately left again next to the bus stop. Take the track past Riverside Cottage and then along a woodland path to the left of the houses. This passes around the back of the museum grounds, with a stone wall on the right. Come to a track crossing the path and keep straight ahead, again next to the wall. The path descends and curves to the right, crossing a stile to meet a road.

**2** Turn right and follow the road for just over 100 yards. Look for a footpath sign on the left hand side of the road. Follow the path just in front of the stone wall of a house. This nicely kept footpath climbs up between houses, crossing a road part of the way up. It arrives by the end of a cul-de-sac, with a big step down to the road! Turn left, passing the end of the cul-de-sac to reach another road. Cross this and find a gap by the side of the gate opposite. Continue on the footpath uphill through the woods. At the top of the hill and just before a boundary wall, a clear earth path turns right through a gap. This follows the top of the small limestone ridge through beech woods, the trees masking a series of disused limestone quarries. After a while the path drops down to meet the road at a kissing gate. Take great care here, as the gate leads straight onto St Fagan's Road, the main road to Cardiff.

**3** Turn left and follow the road for about 200 yards before turning right into Tatem Drive. Soon afterwards turn left into Chorley Close. At the end of this cul-de-sac, turn right, taking a path downhill on the edge of the estate. Pass an electricity substation and continue on a path descending beyond it. Soon arrive at the bottom of the valley, and a junction with a path/cycleway.

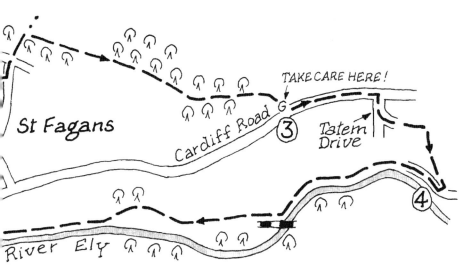

St Fagans

Cardiff Road

TAKE CARE HERE!

③

Tatem Drive

④

River Ely

**4** Turn right, taking the path which passes through woods and meadows alongside the River Ely. *The railway line also uses this valley en route for western Wales.* In about a mile it comes to a road at the bottom of the village of St Fagan's.

**5** To return directly to the start, turn left and in 200 yards, turn right along the museum access road. If you prefer, you could turn right at the end of the cycleway. At the top of the short hill, there is a gatehouse into St Fagan's Castle on the left. *The gate is operated electronically by pressing a buzzer while the castle is open (normally 10.00–17.00).* Go through the gate, pass to the right of the castle and descend a flight of steps. Cross the causeway by the ponds and head back through the grounds to the museum. There are many paths here and it's worth taking some time to meander around the gardens and grounds.

**Blaenwaun Post Office, St Fagan's**

# PRONUNCIATION

| Welsh | English equivalent |
|-------|--------------------|
| c | always hard, as in **cat** |
| ch | as in the Scottish word lo**ch** |
| dd | as th in **then** |
| f | as f in o**f** |
| ff | as ff in o**ff** |
| g | always hard as in **got** |
| ll | no real equivalent. It is like 'th' in then, but with an 'L' sound added to it, giving 'thlan' for the pronunciation of the Welsh 'Llan'. |

In Welsh the accent usually falls on the last-but-one syllable of a word.

## KEY TO THE MAPS

- **➙** Walk route and direction
- Metalled road
- Unsurfaced road
- •••• Footpath/route adjoining walk route
- River/stream
- Trees
- Railway
- **G** Gate
- **S** Stile
- **F.B.** Footbridge
- Viewpoint
- **P** Parking
- **T** Telephone

## THE COUNTRYSIDE CODE

- Be safe – plan ahead and follow any signs
- Leave gates and property as you find them
- Protect plants and animals, and take your litter home
- Keep dogs under close control
- Consider other people

**Open Access**
Some routes cross areas of land where walkers have the legal right of access under The CRoW Act 2000 introduced in May 2005. Access can be subject to restrictions and closure for land management or safety reasons for up to 28 days a year. Details from: www.naturalresourceswales.gov.uk. Please respect any notices.

### Acknowledgements

Thank you to Chris for her patience and diligence transcribing my text – and to Ian for ferrying me around the narrow lanes in this wonderful coastal area.

Published by **Kittiwake-Books Limited**
3 Glantwymyn Village Workshops, Glantwymyn, Machynlleth, Montgomeryshire SY20 8LY

© Text & map research: Alastair Ross 2015
© Maps & illustrations: Kittiwake-Books Ltd 2015
*Drawings by* Morag Perrott
*Cover photos: Main:* Dunraven Bay, Southerndown – David Perrott. *Inset:* St Donats – © Mick Lobb. This work is licensed under the Creative Commons Attribution-Share Alike 2.0 Generic Licence.

Care has been taken to be accurate. However neither the author nor the publisher can accept responsibility for any errors which may appear, or their consequences. If you are in any doubt about access, check before you proceed.

Printed by Mixam, UK.

ISBN: **978 1 908748 24 9**